Taking the Occasion

Taking the Occasion

POEMS

Daniel Brown

WINNER OF THE NEW CRITERION POETRY PRIZE

Ivan R. Dee

CHICAGO 2008

Funding for this year's New Criterion Poetry Prize
has been provided by the Drue Heinz Trust.

www.ivanrdee.com

Library of Congress Cataloging-in-Publication Data:

Brown, Daniel, 1950–
    Taking the occasion : poems / Daniel Brown.
        p. cm. — (Winner of the New Criterion Poetry Prize)
    ISBN-13: 978-1-56663-801-2 (cloth : alk. paper)
    ISBN-10: 1-56663-801-1 (cloth : alk. paper)
    I. Title.
    PS3602.R693T35 2008
    811 '.6—dc22
                        2008032027

For Ellen

Contents

Acknowledgments

The author gratefully acknowledges the following publications in which some of the poems in this book, sometimes in earlier versions, first appeared: *Alaska Quarterly Review*: "Saint Catherine"; *Cream City Review*: "Where I Was"; *The Formalist*: "Epitaph for Deconstruction"; *The New Criterion*: "So Large" (originally appeared as "A Giant"), "Missing It," "Something Like That," "Though Angelless," "Why Do I Exist?"; *Parnassus: Poetry in Review*: "A Window of an Instant," "At Ease"; *Partisan Review*: "In the Chapel in My Head"; *Poetry*: "As Seen at the Uffizi," "Dream after Dream," "Epiphany"; *Tar River Poetry*: "Facing It."

"Missing It" appeared in *The Pushcart Prize XXII: Best of the Small Presses*, edited by Bill Henderson (Pushcart Press).

"As Seen at the Uffizi" appeared in *Fathers: A Collection of Poems*, edited by David Ray (St. Martin's Press).

"Where I Was" appeared in *Poetry 180: A Turning Back to Poetry*, edited by Billy Collins (Random House).

Taking the Occasion

Missing It

The thing about the old one about
The tree in the forest and nobody's around
And how it falls maybe with a sound,
Maybe not, is you throw the part out
About what there isn't or there is,
And the part of it that haunts is still there.
Still there in that the happening, the clear
Crashing there, still encompasses
Everyone condemned to missing it
By being out of the immediate
Vicinity. Out of it the way
You're out of all vicinities but one
All the time — excepting when you've gone
Out of all vicinities to stay.

On Being Asked by Our Receptionist If I Liked the Flowers

"What flowers?" I said. "These flowers," she said,
Gesturing leftward with her head,
And there it was: a vase of flowers
That hadn't graced that fort of hers
The day before. Did I say a vase?
All of an urn is what it was:
Capacious home to a bursting sun
Of thirty lilies if to one.
A splendor I'd have seen for sure,
If less employed in seeing her.

The Greeks

While they certainly had their problems, coming
As they did some thousands of years before
So much that helps the race endure
(Anesthesia, indoor plumbing . . .)
It must have been a kick to be them.
Don't ask me why, but I tend to see them
Strolling along a local shore
In doing their philosophy,
Conceiving truth and tragedy
Among a million notions more . . .
Ah well, can't wind the ages back.
Not that the Greeks were the first to track
Unnumbered prints on continents
Of fresh conceptual terrain.
(I'm thinking of the proto-men
Who named a veldt's constituents.)
There's also reason to suggest
That the Greeks will not have been the last,
Though the next may boast an epochal
Successiveness to men and women;
A character you'd class as human
Hesitantly if at all.

Conundrum

Here's to the tunes
With the brains to hit
Their highest note
Only once,

And the every bit
As brilliant ones
That have the sense
To hammer it.

Something Like That

You know how in Spanish they put
An -ita on things? So this girl
Mildred, this Puerto Rican girl
Where I work, pretty girl—so I get
To thinking that a funny thing about
Her name is that it's one thing that now
That you think of it it isn't clear how
To ita-ize.
                    I'd come right out
And ask her how, but figure it's a bit
Safer to let the questioning begin
With a little in the way of easing in.
As in it is Spanish isn't it
Where they do that, and are we talking small
Things specifically or is it more
Like anything you have affection for
(As if I didn't know already)—all
Of which preliminary inquiries
Get me to the one I'm getting at:
Did they ever call her something like that
When she was a kid?
                              Only lowered eyes.
Then, like something she's confessing to,
That her father did. And would she mind my
Asking what it was? No reply,

So I try a little prompting with a few
Possibilities. Not to press her,
But I've got to know how that would go:
Mildrita? "No." Mildredita? "No."
Mildredecita? "No!" Then . . . "Princesa."

An Aspect of Having Her

Maybe having Alice hasn't
Bettered *everything* — but then,
In a seat on a babe-bedotted bus,
I open to some scandal in

A *Daily News* I'd picked up
(Being in a *News* mood)
And once again experience
An inner glow of gratitude

For one of the many gifts that *have*
Come with having her: my not
Having to worry lest some
Times-type rule me out.

My Own Traces

Dishes sinked, food stowed—
Time for me to hit the road.
A yank at the cord of what
I'd call the kitchen light if this
Nook were more of an excuse
For calling it that.

Whereupon my making for
The freedom of the front door,
In the course of which is when
The awful certainty of my
Never sealing up the rye
Bread steals in.

Nothing but to turn around,
Backtrack to where I find
Myself reentering
The province of the kitchenette,
Only to confront the sight
Of the light-cord aswing.

Not the first case of my
Own traces taking me

Completely by surprise.
Moving me to mutter "So
I *do* exist"—much as though
I'd had it otherwise.

As Seen at the Uffizi

An audience of shepherds
Looks on adoringly
As Mary gently bounces
The babe upon her knee.

To Mary's side stands Joseph.
He isn't looking on.
To judge from his expression
He's wishing he were gone

Well up into the mountains
That rim the little town
To dwell amongst the shepherds
Till things have settled down.

Dream after Dream

All those major league imaginings. . . .
Given the hours I devoted to them,
It's not improper, in the scheme of things,
To take a half a minute to review them.

The steal, the diving catch (to talk about
Kinetic heaven), the going to my right
To glove and wheel and gun the runner out,
The joy of being borne (against the sight

Of thousands of fedoras in the air)
Upon the grateful shoulders of a team
(The Dodgers) from the field (Ebbets) where
I've cleared the wall with one. . . . Dream after dream—

The lot (to state, as now I'm able to,
A truth as patent as a truth can get)
With as good a chance of ever coming true
As certain dreams from earlier. A set

Of fantasies that ran along the lines
Of throwing cars around (thereby waylaying
Many a creep with criminal designs),
Flying planelessly (at times betraying

A light residuum of Super-youth
By veering from my route to pierce a cloud),
Trading cape for tie in a telephone booth,
Stepping from it and melting into the crowd.

Where I Was

I was in Princeton of all
Places. My ninth grade class
Was enduring a tour of the U: a forgettable
Shepherding from edifice
To edifice—no end of gray
Stone—winding up, though,
With something a little out of the way:
The opportunity to view
A classic three-acter
At the U's own theater.

The play I don't remember much
About: a hoary exercise
In wigs and bodices and such.
The memorable thing was
The curtain call. How the one
Coming out was a grim guy
In tweed and tie. How the lone
Lifting of his palm by
Itself extinguished the applause.
How he had "terrible news"—

But not the news I feared. Not
Where to go (to a room below-
Ground). Not how to get

There. Not what to do
There: sit on the floor, put
Your head down, clasp your hands
Behind your head, you might shut
Your eyes in case the world ends—
None of that. Maybe he
Was finding it decidedly

Hard to get the words out,
But what the words amounted to
Wasn't the worst thing: not
Anything that had to do
With going up in a solar hell,
But rather with the President,
A motorcade, a hospital—
With how the evident extent
Of anybody's sudden death
Was elsewhere and over with.

In the Chapel in My Head

Having gone an especially rough round
on the phone with her,
I repaired to the chapel in my head.

Onto whose pew
I'd no sooner settled
than the Lord boiled up by the altar and boomed
"I gave you a tongue.
Abuse it
and I'll pluck it out."

"Hasten the day," I said.

At Ease

It's only a theory, and only a theory's what
It'll probably remain, but were I ever
To get involved with somebody a *lot*
Taller than me, her being so would deliver
The two of us from the tension that attends
On the woman's being only a little taller.
No point in my attempting to make amends
For so great a differential (after all, her
Chin is at the level of my pate)
By some technique—say, straightening up—or other;
A futile effort she'd reciprocate
By slouching? Wearing flats? Why even bother?
What is there for a pair so disparate
In something but to be at ease with it?

A Window of an Instant

I'm striding down the avenue,
And rapidly at that,
When my progress runs me up against
An intersection at

The crux of which, depending from
A stanchion overhead,
An all-commanding traffic light
Presents *two* disks of red:

One to the way that crosses, one
To the way that favors me;
A situation sure to change
Momentarily.

Very little time. But time
Enough for one of those
Windows of an instant with
The power to disclose

Something at my core of cores
(Hence normally unseen)
In my assuming mine's the way
That's not to get the green.

On the Audience's Standing
for the Hallelujah Chorus

A vote for the tradition
Least worthy to be lost
Might go to this: an instance
More visible than most
Of bowing (in our rising)
To the power of the great.
One of those subjections
That only elevate.

The Pass

I've always admired the driving of the guys
Who drive the Greyhound buses. The way the ride
They'll give you can approximate a glide.
No change of speed, or none you'd realize;
As though to prove a given rate can serve
To move a freight of forty souls or so
Some little ways like Butte to Tupelo.
Nor will the least sensation of a swerve
Be registered, not even in a pass.
Here's where the real mastery is seen:
A signaling considerably in
Advance of the move (though not so early as
To be impeachable as premature),
A shifting to the left so gradual
You wouldn't know it's happening at all . . .
And by, with a hint of neither hurry nor
Of hesitance, your highway-liner goes
(Leaving the passed one, whipping right along
He'd thought, to wonder where his life went wrong).
No hurry either in how our driver does
What's left to do (the pass, like many a thing
Performed, not being without its denouement).
Only when he's prudently in front
Of what he's put behind him will he bring
His signal in again, this time to let

Creation in on his intention to
Resume his home in the right hand lane. Which you,
From your perch as passenger, are fortunate
Enough to see him do (that is, see done
With the smooth perfection a professional
Alone commands). A maneuver as a whole,
This pass of his, that doesn't read as one
In the sense of seeming a discrete event;
That rather strikes the traveler as a thing
So well subsumed within the traveling
As to be essentially inevident.
(Though not entirely invisible
To anyone with eyes to see its wake in
Some fifty miles of the overtaken.)
Clearly something learned. Perhaps as well
The star perfection of an artisan
(If one whose works are written on the air)
Natively unable to forbear
From working such perfections as he can.

Taking the Occasion

As if her grace were not enough,
Her taking the occasion of
A trip across the kitchen floor
To lift into tiptoe-
And-pirouette: a *prima* mo-
Mentarily forevermore.

Epiphany

At moments it can seem as though
The thoughts I'm thinking in
Shouldn't merely be described
As no thoughts of mine
But no thoughts at all—not
If intellect implies
Something less suggestive of
A tripping of relays.

It's one thing to entertain
A notion of the self
As a chimera constructed from
Components off the shelf,
Another thing entirely
To have the truth of this
As present to the sentience as
Your hand before your face.

Granted this epiphany,
I'm not inclined to blame
The moment when it dissipates
As quickly as it came.
Nor to blame myself for seeing

Nothing to deplore
In the matter of its not having
Changed things more.

Facing It

I rarely think of genius of
The math variety without
Finding myself thinking about
An episode I had to love.

It happened back in college. I
Was crossing the quad early one
Evening—maybe no sun
Anymore, but still a sky

To speak of, if not to go
On about: the ritual
Indigo of nightfall—
Crossing, as I say, when who

Should happen to be approaching on
An intersect course but one
Eigenmeyer, i.e., the one
Genius-level mathematician

Among us undergrads, I'd been
Creditably told. A guy
I maybe knew to say hi
To. Not a friend of mine

Or anything. . . . So here it is,
A chance for us to reaffirm
This state of affairs for another term.
Each of us emitting his

"Hi." At least one of us
Wondering exactly what
There was to do beyond that,
When—listen: are we hearing geese?

A honking barely there—but that's
All it takes to get the eye
Directed to the northern sky . . .
A hundred plus, we're looking at.

Obvious believers in
The V-ness of getting there,
Relative to going air-
Wise. All coming on

Toward us riveted
Ones. . . . Damn clamorous
In passing on over us. . . .
Whence the V of them proceed

To trail a sorrow every bit
The blessing jubilation is,
In passing on away. And as
For Eigenmeyer: as for what

If anything there was to say
To such a one at such a time—

Perhaps you'll pardon me if I'm
Proud of how my digging way

Down enabled me to come
Up with something apropos.
To wit, did Eigenmeyer know
That somehow or other some

Sort of bird or other'd been
Shown to count as high as eight?
He answers that he would have thought
Nine. I ask him why nine.

He says I wouldn't understand:
With nothing you could call conceit,
Nothing you could call regret.
Tell me I'm supposed to mind.

Among the Better Blessings

Among the better blessings there's
The blessedness of knowing
That vision, skin, body, brain
Have all started going.

For how it is with death is how
It is with anything:
Easier to accept when it's
Already happening.

Though Angelless

I once glanced up at a tree and found it full of angels
singing praises to God.
—Blake

If I'm to take this visionary quote
As something of a challenge (not a bad
Way of taking everything he wrote)
It isn't one I'd be exactly glad
To tackle. *Angels* thronged those wild eyes!
The realist in me would settle for
The gleam (to name a consolation prize)
That Wordsworth was at pains to say he saw
In nature (as a kid at least), but this,
If it ever lent its lucence to my view,
Has been long since retired to the shelf.
Which doesn't mean a tree, though angelless,
Won't move me now and then to loose a few
Notes of praise from the old throat myself.

I'm Better Now

Back when I was new at falling for,
My fantasies would leap excessively
Ahead: to, say, my sitting by her bed
Some day, hand squeezing aged hand goodbye.

I'm better now, if better means that my
Imaginings of love now leap ahead
Even beyond her slamming of a door
To my being fine (at worst) with losing her.

A Job for Ockham's Razor

From the annals of Fifth Ave (right
In front of the Library). They
Hadn't taken the grandstand
Down from some Day the day

Before. What was funny was
The extent to which the thing was still
Occupied—as though its mere
Presence made it capable

Of peopling itself. There
Were as many as fifty or so of us
At any rate, all taking
In the scene, such as

It was: not yesterday's
Respectable parade, just
The usual unruly one.
A good fifty or so, most

Of whom presumably had paused,
In the course of a busy afternoon,
To clamber up and settle down
And wave it all serenely on.

I liked that. Liked how,
Given a nice place to sit,
A body of souls was sitting there,
Whatever obligations not

Withstanding. Not that *I* had
A lot to do, but it looked as though
Enough of the others probably did:
Suits and white shirts and so

Forth. And yet what they
Amounted to was nothing less
Than a village of the idle in
A city of the sedulous.

Sure, it shook my view a bit
When half the villagers or more
Went storming down as one upon
The pulling up of an M-4

Bus. But there was the other half.
The half that happened to survive.
The half that lasted all the way
To the pulling up of an M-5.

Since He Asked

O what am I that I should not seem
For the song's sake a fool?
—Yeats

Not to say what, but that strain
Of his that seems the singing of a loon:
Were it capable of helping us to bear
Reality's considerable weight—
To say this much is to despair
Of ever asking it to do that.

I grant you he could be more wrong
With reference to imperishable song.
Grant you that the fashioning of such
Is often done, even only done,
At fever pitch—and yet a fever pitch
Of reason if the truth be known.

Beshadowed

Why this one landing out of the hundreds I'd
Survived was being shown on the overhead
TV in the plane, who knew? Enough that it was
(As captured by a camera in the nose
It must have been, given the screen's presenting
A dead-on view of what we were descending
Toward). Enough to savor this surprise
Sight of things as from the pilot's eyes:
Of the drome as a whole (though it was only dusk
The field's lights already a luciplex)
And a strip that as we neared looked more and more
Like our destination in particular.
The one most memorable element
Was a plane preceding us in its descent.
Not to say I wasn't seeing rather—
The dusk does funny things—my aged mother
Returning to earth (or so it struck a son,
Himself beshadowed, following her down).

The Way It Is

I'm not the most observant guy
To say the least. If I tell you I
Could pass a boulder in the hall
Secure in my habitual
Oblivion, you needn't doubt it.
Although to be fair to myself about it,
A nipple-hint in a blouse or dress
Is a little thing I've yet to miss.

Water Lilies

I'd be lying if I told you I
remember the particular
that triggered it: perhaps a gray-
green sprinkle of stipple suddenly under-
stood as a reflection of
a branch's leaves . . . or maybe a re-
gion of chalky blue—a kind of hov-
er of it—seen belatedly
as pond-embodied sky. . . . Whatever
did it, what I found that I
was walking along (more gliding over
is how it felt, like a dragonfly)
was not an abstract-fantasy-
inspired-by, as it had seemed,
but rather a surprisingly
literal (if partly dreamed)
depiction of the surface of
a lily pond. Of its depths as well
(beneath the mirrored darks of the grove
a darker, like an underknell). . . .
Of the lily flowers (one really should-
n't omit their kilovolt vermil-
lionness, as if description could). . . .
Of (just as unomissible)
the clouds, like pours of colored powder

(peach and rose and variants)
severally blooming in the water
(purples, mints . . .). The painting's dance
of tinctured drifts and daubs and all
as purely dance? Extremely nice.
But see the real in it—you'll
have had a brush with paradise.

Gossamer

More years and more,
Till it's gotten to where
When a certain face at times re-
Surfaces in my mind's eye,
It's incomplete.
Parts of it
Have turned to air.
              A word that
Might be applied to that of it
That does appear
Is "gossamer,"
The way my view of wherever I am
Is showing through.
              There was a time
When the more I sought
To shake the sight,
The more it seemed impossible
Not to see and see in all
Its loveliness
This fading face.

Saint Catherine

The first I saw of her
was a foot the size of a child's.
It was sitting, if a foot
can be said to sit,
in a glass case on a pedestal.
Whoever had severed it
had brought it off neatly:
a clean cleave at the ankle.
Was that faint streak descending from the cut
a ghost of sainted blood?
My *Guide to the Churches of Venice*
was untypically mum.

Her head,
on its shelf in Siena,
bespoke a comely face: good bones
beneath the papery skin.
I didn't love the way she had her hair—
those hangdog locks
needed a flip or something—
but at least she had it.
Her lips were a different story.

Her body? Out of sight
in a sealed tomb I stood before in Rome.

Epitaph for Deconstruction

A puff of wind that really shouldn't
Have blown so many so far astray—
And yet not anyone who wouldn't
Have come to nothing anyway.

A Cockfight Dance

I was heading up the office aisle one morning
When I overheard a guy from the Philippines
Saying he used to dance professionally.
Hard to credit, what with the belly on him,
Though the revelation did make sudden sense
Of a gait you couldn't miss the music in.
I ventured over to have a look at the proof
He'd pulled from his wallet: a snap of him performing
In a folk-dance troupe back home (no belly there).
While his shirt and pants in the shot were standard issue
(If entirely white), you couldn't say the same
For the long green feathers dangling from his arms.
On the evidence of a jagged comb of red
You were looking at a rooster. What he called it
Was a cock. As in a fighting cock. The dance
Was a cockfight dance. (An adversary, he told us,
Was lurking slightly out of camera range.)
No sooner did someone suggest a demonstration
Than a fowl was in the house, kicking and pecking
And otherwise being lethal. A glimpse of no-
Kidding visitation—whereupon,
Panting, a man again. Among the ensuing
Kudos was a crack to the effect
That if that was how he'd danced a cockfight dance
He must have won. Some evenings he, some evenings

The other guy, he said. For variety
You'd think, or for the sake of fair is fair,
But why speculate when he shared the real reason
He and his partner shuffled things like that:
To give two stagehand friends of theirs the pleasure
Of bouts that could accommodate a bet.

A Salmon Speaks of the Sea

You approach it
with an image of it
but nothing prepares you for it.

Shot with sun in its upper reaches,
a bankless realm dims in descent,
gradually devolving toward a blackness
one fins through life
trying not to think about.

Yet up from that nethernight
jut those peaks and ridges
that provide so much of the grandeur here.
Much of the interest, too,
their faces being
very carnivals of incident.
Especially compelling
are those dramas it's healthier
to witness than to live.
How some of them stay with me!
Like that silverlittle's despondent swim
right down the throat of an anemone:
as though loveloss
had crushed it past caring.
Never more finally

has a clutch of red wormicles
closed over its hole.

And yet . . .
the giant fans,
slow-asway
in the waterwind . . .
the manta ray,
its glide a thing
of a ripple of wing . . .
the jellyfish,
that opened out
heart of light . . .
in singing these sublimities,
I ask the several
to stand for the innumerable.

Such richesse!
The river was nice
but never like this.
I have no intention
of ever getting over it.

"Why Do I Exist?"

Answer it? Nobody can
(To go by the hordes that haven't yet).
But as for having the question down,
You know you're really asking it
When it isn't merely answerless
But answerless in the strongest sense:
Answerless in being less
A question than an utterance.

The Birth of God

It happened near Lascaux
Millions of dawns ago.
For dawn it was,
Infusing radiance
And cuing avians
The way it does,

That saw the two of them
(Odds are a her and him,
Though maybe not)
Emerging from the mouth
Of a cave a couple south
Of the one that's got

All that painted fauna
All but snorting on a
Wall. That is
To say, from the mouth of a cave
Unconsecrated save
By the sighs and cries

Of the night just past. The pair
Has borne the bliss they share
Out into the bright.
Where silently they stand

Thanking, hand in hand
Before the light.

Their gratitude is truly
New beneath the duly
Erupting sun.
A gratitude that so
Wants a place to go
It authors one.

Prayer

Repeatedly
A new house
Larger than
The previous —

In each case
The previous
Persisting as
A part of us —

This growth as
Of the nautilus
May our selves
Suffer us.

Love Story

1.
What does it say
that of everyone I've known
the one I want to talk about
is the prof I took my first theory from
(theory as in music theory)?

2.
His name (to limit him
to his last, as he did with us)
was Morrison.
A little guy,
typically in tweed,
checkered vest, bow tie . . .
Nice enough looking—
you didn't have to be queer per se
to want to touch the waves
of his dark brown, brilliantined hair—
though his best feature
may have been a rich baritone
subtly engruffed with the smoke
of constant Kools.

3.

His big, handsome,
honey-blond wife (dwarfed Morrison)
was a small-time mezzo I took
some voice lessons from.
Not many; just enough
for the two of us to realize we liked
gassing together too much
ever to get anywhere.
Before she was his wife she'd been his student
at a women's college down south.
I remember her telling me
that whenever he was up in front of her class
"there wasn't a dry seat in the house."

4.

Early on he was explaining
what a key is. Likening
the downward tug of the tonic
to the pull of gravity.
All very interesting,
though I was especially taken
with his observation, *passim*,
that pieces in C
invariably return
to "C level."

5.

In handing our nightly
harmonizations back,
he'd make a point, not to say a rite,
of reading out the grades.
Including an F or two usually;

these delivered
with all the gruff he could muster.
My classmate Young and I,
we thought those "F!"s
were the funniest vocables going;
would loose their like at each other
whenever we ran into one another.
Young was even lucky enough
to absorb a few of the real things.
As for me—
I still remember
handing in something that broke
most every rule in our harmony book
(this being Art I was up to).
Next morning . . .
"Miss Cotton, B.
Mr. Randle, A-minus.
Mr. Brown . . . Ah, Mr. Brown.
So many no-no's, Mr. Brown.
And yet to speak of the rules of harmony
is to speak of what genius did
'as a rule.'
Infraction with cause is permissible.
And these infractions of yours, Mr. Brown:
They leave me no choice but to award you
the grade . . . of . . .
F!!"

6.
Happening past the campus
chapel one day,
I heard a wraith of organ coming from it.
Ambled up the walk,

tugged open the door. . . .
A lesson he was giving
Randle. I saw Morrison see me
as I slipped into the choir loft to listen.
"*Flauto* would be a little
obvious here," he was saying.
"Though being obvious
doesn't necessarily make it wrong."
A point he supported
by pulling a stop and wafting a few bars.
"*Hautbois* is also possible. . . .
Now that one hears it, very possible.
Any preference, John?"
John?
Who was Randle to get to be John?
From whom, in the event,
nothing in reply.
"And you, Dan."
Dan!
"Which would you choose?"
The best I could manage was the truth:
that they both sounded good.
"Yes," he mused,
"they both are good . . .
but different.
And if they're different, one
must be better, yes?"
Twenty years,
and the question's still right where he hung it
in the musty air.

7.
I passed that course,
and on to Theory 2 with Prof 2,
and didn't see nearly as much of him. . . .
Though I did join the choir, which he conducted,
and sang for him for the rest of my time there.
For a while after,
I'd hear of him from Young (who'd stayed on
for Law). Seemed he'd started
appearing around campus
in open-necked shirts and gold chains—
and then had stopped appearing. Rumor had it
he was off drying out somewhere.
(Young claimed to have suspected from the first;
something about the way
he'd drawn on those Kools.)
By the time he'd returned,
his wife had followed a graduating voice major
even unto Queens, two
kids in tow. Last I heard,
he was back at his several stands,
sans the chains but still with the open shirts.
Me, I tend to see him
in his tweedier incarnation,
as he was rehearsing the choir one morning
(if without his jacket)
in Carissimi's *Jephte*.
We were working on its great closing
chorus of lamentation
when it came to me,
in my perch well up in the tenors,
to put an especially hard *c*

on the *carmine* in *carmine dolorem*.
It cracked like a rifle shot.
In its gruffness cutting
with equal ease through the whole curtain of sound,
up came his muttered "Marvelous!"

So Large

Big world when I was very young.
The shopping aisles a mile long . . .
Our lawn, though anything but wide,
Unfolding like a countryside . . .
The sky! So large and far away . . .
Exactly as it is today.

Deliverance

When I think about how
We deal with our mortality
I think about a sense in which it's like we
Deal with an injury.

About how, on first
Comprehending the ultimate
Hurt, we harrow it more nights than not:
This at the behest of that

Cave-old, even
Ocean-old imperative
To reckon at its maximally grave
Any injury we have.

How, years having passed,
We find ourselves assessing it
Far less frequently, and more by rote
Than necessity: our purpose not

To sound the wound so much as
To remind ourselves it's still there.
How one day we're suddenly aware
Of its no longer being there.

Daniel Brown's poems have appeared in *Poetry*, *Partisan Review*, *Parnassus: Poetry in Review*, *The New Criterion*, and other journals. Winner of a Pushcart Prize, he has been widely anthologized in volumes such as *Poetry 180*, edited by Billy Collins, and *Fathers*, edited by David Ray. He holds a masters degree in musicology from Cornell University and has taught at Cornell and Dartmouth College. His *Why Bach?*, an appreciation of Bach's music, is available on the Internet. He lives in Baldwin, New York.